The love that you gave me from the moment I was born
has given me the strength and confidence to share my love by

_____

_____

_____

_____

_____

_____

_____

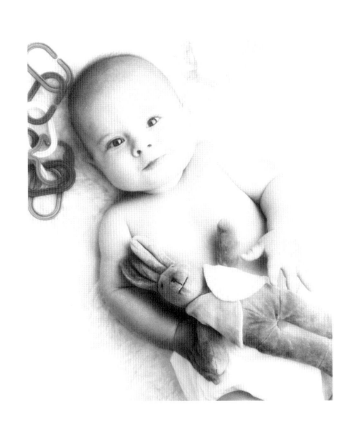

I remember a time when I didn't feel lovable,
but you loved me anyway

_____

_____

_____

_____

_____

_____

_____

_____

The feeling of security is within me today and is felt when I

_____

_____

_____

_____

_____

_____

_____

_____

I remember happiness in this way

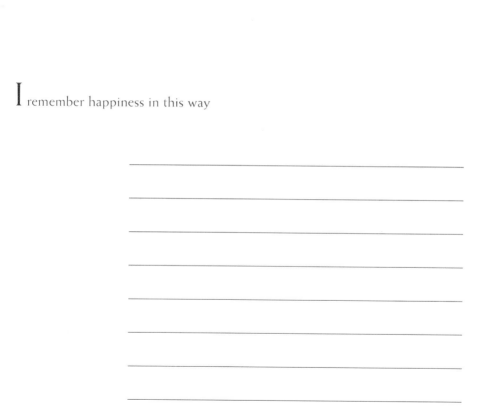

It took endless patience to

_____

_____

_____

_____

_____

_____

_____

_____

I can remember so many of them. One of my favorites is

_____

_____

_____

_____

_____

_____

_____

_____

You have nourished me in the wisdom of

_____

_____

_____

_____

_____

_____

_____

_____

I remember your voice delighting me in my earliest years when you

_____

_____

_____

_____

_____

_____

_____

_____

You taught me the importance of keeping a sense of humor through the most trying of times. Like the time that

_____

_____

_____

_____

_____

_____

_____

You showed me that discipline was more important than anger when you

_____

_____

_____

_____

_____

_____

_____

_____

The birthday that I remember most vivdly is

_____

_____

_____

_____

_____

_____

_____

_____

This is what I would like to tell you now.

Without you I never would have accomplished

_____

_____

_____

_____

_____

_____

_____

I will never forget

_____

_____

_____

_____

_____

_____

_____

_____

My favorite memory of our home is

_____

_____

_____

_____

_____

_____

_____

_____

You weren't afraid to let me

_____

_____

_____

_____

_____

_____

_____

Those were the days I was growing and learning and here is one lesson I learned

_____

_____

_____

_____

_____

_____

_____

_____

Remember when you coached me to be

_____

_____

_____

_____

_____

_____

_____

Being in the outdoors has meant to me

_____

_____

_____

_____

_____

_____

_____

_____

Remember when you

_____

_____

_____

_____

_____

_____

_____

_____

You taught me patience as we worked through one project after another like this one

_____

_____

_____

_____

_____

_____

_____

With your help I discovered that

_____

_____

_____

_____

_____

_____

_____

The times we were all together live on in my mind as the best of times. One of my favorite is

_____

_____

_____

_____

_____

_____

_____

_____

I remember your loving advice when I

_____

_____

_____

_____

_____

_____

_____

You have a talent for

_____

_____

_____

_____

_____

_____

_____

I remember a time so clearly when your suggestion of

_____

_____

_____

_____

_____

_____

_____

_____

I didn't know it then, but now I know

_____

_____

_____

_____

_____

_____

_____

_____

Of all my ambitions and dreams you were always there for

_____

_____

_____

_____

_____

_____

_____

_____

You have shown me how to live by

_____

_____

_____

_____

_____

_____

_____

Without you my life would have been so empty. I became
aware of this when

_____

_____

_____

_____

_____

_____

_____

_____

You opened my eyes to the larger world when you

_____

_____

_____

_____

_____

_____

_____

_____